I0151020

Great Athlete

Blueprint of a Great Athlete

Table of Contents

Blueprint of a Great Athlete

Blueprint of a Great Athlete

Blueprint of a Great Athlete

Donovan Davis
5036 Dr. Phillips Blvd. Suite 124
Orlando, Florida 32819

Blueprint of a Great Athlete
First Edition
2025 by Donovan Davis

ISBN: 978-09802391-4-0

Blueprint of a Great Athlete

Acknowledgments

First I would like to thank my lord and savior Jesus Christ for inspiring me to write this book. Second, I'll be honest; it is hard for me to write acknowledgments for the simple reason that my life as a father has been blessed with a multitude of parental influences. Of course, I have to begin with the love of my life Marquita. We've been together for some time now and have shared some great times together. To my children Desire and Destiny, you girls are growing up so fast, and I love you both dearly. To my mother I miss you dearly and I wish you could be here to enjoy this accomplishment. I love you always and I know you are watching over me.

Special thanks to my fraternity brothers the men of Phi Beta Sigma Fraternity, Inc. and Zeta Phi Beta Sorority, Inc.

To some of my mother's closest friends Lillie Thomas, Mildred Singleton, and Mary McCloud who are all excellent parents, thank you for being a positive and influential guide of what true parenting is all about.

The Thomas family, the McCloud, the Singleton family, the Rolle family, the Johnson family, the Lumpkin family, and the Decembert family.

Blueprint of a Great Athlete

If I didn't mention someone please don't take it personal, blame it on the head, and not the heart. Thank you to Vincent Palmer for an awesome web site www.askdonovandavis.com

Good Person

Great Athlete

Self- Esteem Section

Blueprint of a Great Athlete

Self Esteem Section

Self- Esteem- is the ability to feel good about ourselves whether or not we are always. Successful it is a feeling of satisfaction we experience after our needs are met.

How does self esteem affect me as a great athlete?

We as athletes can help build our own self-esteem by telling our self positive things. Parents can help by praising their little athletes for good decisions, small deeds and great initiatives. Parents must also acknowledge their child's potential

What does communication have to do with building self-esteem?

Communication is the key to success in any relationship. It's no different in building the self-esteem in athletes.

Blueprint of a Great Athlete

Hearing I love you helps build athletes self esteem. Therefore, that is why it is imperative to receive compliments from adult authority figures on how we look and how smart we are.

Resolving Conflict Section

Blueprint of a Great Athlete

Resolving Conflict Section

The next important phase of development within a great athlete is being able to resolve conflict without violence and confrontation. Unfortunately, athletes often allow anger to control them when a conflict arises. Athletes will naturally lash out if they are annoyed or openly criticized by coaches or authority figures. A small conflict can affect a relationship forever if it isn't resolved properly.

Blueprint of a Great Athlete

When there is a conflict athletes must learn how to deal with them properly, below is a list of things we SHOULD NOT do:

1. Not listen

2. Blaming, insults

3. Not taking responsibility

4. Threats, cursing

5. Physically hitting

.

Blueprint of a Great Athlete

The list of things we SHOULD do if the conflict is arises:

1. Recognize what the problem is.

2. Attack the problem.

3. Care about others feelings.

4. Be responsible for a positive outcome to the conflict.

Athletes must learn strategies to resolve conflict on their own.

Blueprint of a Great Athlete

Three Strategies for Resolving Conflict

Share what ever it is and they will understand that feelings are more important than things.

Compromise athletes must learn at a young age about compromise.

Apologize- athletes should learn when they are wrong that it is ok to apologize.

Decision Making Section

Blueprint of a Great Athlete

Decision Making Section

Unfortunately, athletes can't be around their parents all day, so we have to be able to make decisions on our own. The decisions we as athletes make may affect our lives forever. Great athletes identify the consequences that must be considered.

Great athletes will encounter situations where we are approached to participate in "unproductive or dangerous" activities. And because we all want to be accepted and have friends sometimes we will give in and sometimes we take a stance to do what was right. However, it is essential to remember and relate to this feeling in order to help stay out of trouble.

Blueprint of a Great Athlete

Eight Step Decision Making Model

Step- 1   Recognize what the situation is.

Step-2   Who is involved in the situation?

Step-3   What are the two choices in the situation?

Step-4   What are the positive consequences of choice one?

Step-5   What are the negative consequences of choice one?

Step-6   What are the positive consequences of choice two?

Step-7   What are the negative consequences of choice two?

Step-8   After attempting to think through all of the previous steps then we can make an informed decision.

Blueprint of a Great Athlete

If we as athletes use even part of the eight steps it will help us make better decisions. We must always think before we make decisions.

Blueprint of a Great Athlete

Problem:

You suspect your buddy of using drugs. The first step is to identify the symptoms. Laziness, mood swings, change in eating habits, and change in peer group.

Step-2 Consider their friends behavior that they associate with on a daily basis.

Step-3 The two choices in this situation are:

Choices #1 search your friend's car while they aren't looking for drugs.

Choice #2 ask your friend directly if they are doing drugs.

Step-4 The positive consequences of searching your friend's car is you find the drugs and you can help them get help.

Blueprint of a Great Athlete

Step-5 The negative consequence of searching your friend's car is you don't find anything. Immediately you will feel guilty about snooping around in their car.

Step-6 The positive consequences of asking directly if they are using drugs is they could tell you the truth and the answer is no.

Step-7 The negative consequences of asking directly if they are using drugs. They could lie or say yes and continue to use drugs.

Step-8 Make a decision.

Goal Setting Section

Blueprint of a Great Athlete

Goal Setting Section

The next section of this book is on Goal Setting. We have a responsibility to our selves to set goals. We must also understand that there are two types of goals short and long-term goals.

Types of Goals

Short Term Goals- are goals that you plan on reaching within a month or less.

Long Term Goals- are goals that you plan on reaching within the next few months or even years.

The importance of setting goals is crucial to our success. Great athletes who do not have goals eventually lack purpose in their lives and may never develop their true talents and abilities.

Blueprint of a Great Athlete

Now that we have addressed the different types of goals, the next step is to address how to set goals. There are five steps that will help you as an athlete on how to set goals.

Five Steps to Goal Setting

Step-1   Define what you really want to do.

Step-2   Decide what steps you must take to achieve the goal.

Step-3   Think of what obstacles could get in the way of you achieving your goal.

Step-4   Think of ways of overcoming your possible obstacles.

Step-5   Set a deadline for each of your goals.

Blueprint of a Great Athlete

Keys to Reaching Goals

Key #1 Self Discipline- you must be willing to focus and work on your goal whether you feel like it or not daily.

Key #2 Commitment- you must be willing to work towards attaining your goal on a consistent basis.

Key #3 Sacrifice- you may have to give up something like your time or your focus to get your goal.

When these three elements are applied and practiced us as athletes can reach any realistic goal.

Discipline

Blueprint of a Great Athlete

What are discipline and the goals of discipline?

•Discipline means teaching and training.

The Goals of Good Discipline:

•To encourage appropriate behavior.

•To help prevent problems from arising

•To instill a lifelong sense of self-discipline.

Why is discipline important?

•Discipline is the key to the way you will behave.

Why should I focus on discipline today?

•Appropriate and consistent discipline can make life smoother and more pleasant for you.

Blueprint of a Great Athlete

Discipline is an on going process!!

•It begins early in the child's life.

•It involves changes as the child matures.

•It continues until the child is an adult, and then goes on as self-discipline.

How does discipline help the development of a great athlete?

Discipline helps athletes with:

1. Develop self-control

2. Express emotions appropriately

3. Respect others' rights

4. Build self-esteem

5. Become self-reliant

6. Develop orderliness

Blueprint of a Great Athlete

Developing Self-Control

• Feelings of anger, jealousy, helplessness and fear are only natural at times. They may surface as temper tantrums, whining or fighting.

Express Emotions Appropriately

• It's not always easy to say "I'm sorry" or "That hurt my feelings." Talking about feelings can help prevent misunderstanding and bitterness.

Respect Others' Rights

• Everyone has the right to privacy, to be spoken to politely and to have personal belongings left alone.

• Build Self-Esteem

• Athletes need attention and praise when they show good sportsmanship. This helps reinforce good feelings about themselves.

Blueprint of a Great Athlete

Become Self-Reliant

• Athletes need to learn how to take care of themselves (dress, wash, etc.) and to do simple household tasks. Mastering these skills helps great athletes develop confidence in their abilities.

Develop Orderliness

• Good work habits help athletes succeed at sports, at school and, as an adult, at work. We can't excuse repeated forgetfulness, messiness as part of our personality.

Blueprint of a Great Athlete

Four Areas of Misbehavior

There are four areas that may be the cause of misbehavior:

➢ Anger

➢ Hurt

➢Fear

➢Jealousy

Anger

•Athletes may become angry when they don't get what they want. If parents or authority figures give in to angry demands, the athlete learns that anger "works" and will continue to use it.

Blueprint of a Great Athlete

Hurt

•Feelings of hurt or disappointment can linger for a long time.

•Fear

•Great athletes have a fear of failure. Sometimes their actions are misinterpreted as deliberate misbehavior.

Jealousy

•They may use misbehavior to get attention.

Behavior and Character

Blueprint of a Great Athlete

Character traits athletes and coaches should display?

1. Trustworthiness - athletes should be honest, promise-keepers, courageous, and loyal people.

2. Respect - athletes should be polite, appreciates others, considerate, and is an open-minded person.

3. Responsibility - athletes should take on the responsibility of becoming excellent worker, goal setter, reliable worker, and be a good example.

4. Fairness - athletes should be good listeners, an understanding friend, be a good sport, and be a just decision-maker.

5. Caring - athletes should share, help others, display kindness towards others, and be a person who does well to everyone.

6. Citizenship - athletes should follow rules, be good neighbors, take care of the environment, and volunteer your time.

Blueprint of a Great Athlete

Trust

As a coach, your primary goals within athletics should be to build character, self-esteem, teamwork, leadership, teach the fundamentals of the sport, teach the rules associated with the sport, and have fun playing the sport. You should encourage athletes to focus on the meaning and the importance of trustworthiness within your particular sport. Athletes must adopt a policy of being honest and demanding honesty from teammates, their parents, and coaching staff. Make it a point to not engage in or permit dishonesty by lying, deception, or trickery by any means. Be willing to admit your mistakes openly and honestly as a demonstration of your integrity. Keep your commitments by doing what you say. Evaluate your rules on a regular basis with your team members (coaches, athletes, and parents) and ask yourself and others whether

each is following these rules.

Blueprint of a Great Athlete

Respect

Coaches, athletes, and their parents must always treat the players, referees, opposing players and their fans with respect, courtesy, and consideration. This means avoiding and preventing put-downs, name calling, trash-talking, insults, or other verbal or non-verbal conduct. It also means never taunting an opponent or engaging in flamboyant displays of chest-thumping, ball-slamming, or high-fiving. Coaches, athletes, and their parents must be informed that if they think an official misunderstands a rule or made a bad call, they should not humiliate the referee through their own behavior. Coaches need to maintain control over the conduct of their parents, fans, and players by preventing negative cheers, name-calling, trash talking, or the like. It should be emphasized that demeaning, ridiculing, yelling at, or embarrassing players for their mistakes or for any other reason will not be tolerated. Treat all of your players as you would like to be treated, recognizing and appreciating their diversity in gender, ethnicity, skills, and race as a part of good sportsmanship and respect. And finally, emphasize that everyone associated with the team will be listened to for their input and opinions without fear of reprisal or put down.

Blueprint of a Great Athlete

Responsibility

Responsibility means accepting that you have control over your thoughts, actions, and feelings. It means recognizing that you have the power to make both good choices and poor choices. It means being accountable for the consequences of your actions.

Responsible people are dependable; they fulfill their obligations and do what needs to be done; they don't make excuses for their mistakes; they always use good judgment; they exercise self- control.

As a coach, athlete, or parent of an athlete, you should never lose your temper, throw things, scream, or exhibit uncontrolled anger at any time. You should focus on demonstrating good sportsmanship always. You should make it a point to win with dignity and also lose with dignity.

Blueprint of a Great Athlete

Fairness

Fairness means treating others the way you want to be treated. Fair-minded people play by the rules and don't take advantage of others. As the leader of a sports program you should teach and model what fair play is. Make sure that your team plays honorably; be open to input and ideas from others; be evenhanded and reasonable in your decision-making; consider the feelings of all people who will be affected by your actions and decisions; treat all players with impartiality.

Blueprint of a Great Athlete

Caring

Athletes are, first and foremost, role models; they are among the most influential people in a young athlete's life. Because coaches are such powerful role models, young athletes learn more from them about character than about athletic performance. Coaches, who truly care about their athletes and show it by treating them in caring ways, are actually teaching these kids how to be caring people, themselves. Caring people are responsive to the concerns and needs of others. They treat people with kindness, concern, and generosity. They are charitable, giving of themselves unselfishly for the benefit of others. And they are never mean, cruel, or insensitive. Coaches can model caring behavior by taking a genuine and continual interest in each athlete as a person. Coaches should willingly counsel, advise, encourage and console without regard to athletic performance, and become knowledgeable about support programs for athletes that address academic, emotional, and social issues that may arise. They should teach and model kindness and compassion for others, and they should teach and demand teamwork and discourage selfishness. Caring is one of the pillars of good character.

Blueprint of a Great Athlete

Citizenship

Being a good citizen is not developed through mere participation in sports. Citizenship is, at its core, social responsibility. It means doing your part for the common good, making your community and its institutions work well, serving the community, and obeying the laws. Citizenship through athletic participation occurs both on and off the playing surface, both in and out of season. Developing good citizen-athletes involves defining and developing the relationship from athlete to athlete, from athlete to team and from athlete to community. Connecting athletes to the community should be an important part of any athletic program. A coach may remind the athletes that the community supports them through taxes and through attendance at events, and that they have an obligation to give back to the community in some way. The community is part of their team, and its role should not go unacknowledged.

Good Sport Conduct

Blueprint of a Great Athlete

What is Good Sport Conduct?

Good sport conduct is the behaviors appropriate of a sport participant. In other words, coaches should teach their athletes to "treat others, as you would like to be treated." Episodes of coaches, parents, and athletes behaving poorly at sporting events are often reported in newspapers and on television.

Examples of good sport conduct include:

- shaking hands with opponents after a game

- helping an opponent up after a play

- showing concern for injured opponents

- accepting all decisions of the referees

- encouraging less skilled teammates

Blueprint of a Great Athlete

- congratulating an excellent effort by opponents

Examples of poor sport conduct includes:

- trash talking

- causing injury to an opponent on purpose

- cheating

- making fun of teammates' effort, skill, race/ethnicity, or size

- blaming losses on others

- running up the score against your opponents

Blueprint of a Great Athlete

Model Good Sport Conduct

There are many ways that you can teach kids good conduct; the best way is for you to model good sport conduct.

Young players look to their coaches as role models and are likely to observe their coaches' behaviors. It is unlikely that athletes will be able to control their behaviors, if their coaches are unable to control their own behavior. Coaches who show respect to officials and opponents before, during, and after games can truly expect their players to do the same.

Examples of showing respect to officials

- avoid calling the officials names

Blueprint of a Great Athlete

- civilly question calls

- be open to idea that the official is correct

- put yourself in the official's shoes

Examples of showing respect to opponents

- give your best coaching effort

- celebrate victory respectfully

- engage in the pre- and post-game handshake

- give credit to opponents

During practices and games, it is imperative that coaches remain under control during interactions with players, assistant coaches, officials, and opposing coaches. Parents observing the good conduct of their children's coach will soon understand the responsibility they have

to engage in good sport conduct as spectators.

Blueprint of a Great Athlete

All coaches should encourage athletes to reflect on their behaviors by asking them questions. One discussion format that could be used is as follows.

1. identify the problem

2. identify negative and positive actions

3. identify how each action influences people involved

4. choose best action

- Reward athletes on your team who behave as good sports. Discipline athletes who behave as poor sports. By allowing poor sport conduct to happen on your team, you are teaching athletes that poor sport conduct is acceptable.

Blueprint of a Great Athlete

- Teach athletes to be considerate of their teammates and their opponents when they win and lose.

- Emphasize respecting opponents and officials whether they win or lose.

- Stress the importance of good sportsmanship at parent meetings.

- Make sure your athletes know and follow the rules of the sport.

When a superstar athlete misbehaves, his antics make headlines and TV news everywhere—including, most likely, in your house. Your child gets a lesson in sportsmanship, whether you like it or not. And it probably isn't the kind of lesson you like.

Blueprint of a Great Athlete

Not surprisingly, as bad sportsmanship becomes more prevalent on the pro level, it seems to be more common on junior levels as well.

Guidance for parents and their kids

Blueprint of a Great Athlete

WINNING IS EVERYTHING

Why can't athletes behave? The prime obstacle, according to sports psychologists, is the win-at-all-cost attitude many parents and coaches—and our culture, in general—instill in kids. Even adults who try to teach kids that "its how you play the game that matters" are hard-pressed to compete with advertisements that tell youngsters' winning is everything.

What can parents and coaches do to instill notions of fair play and good sportsmanship in children? Plenty, say sports psychologists. Here's some advice from four experts to whom we spoke.

Blueprint of a Great Athlete

STANDARDS AND CONSEQUENCES

Set clear standards of behavior and enforce them with a system of consequences. Let the coach know that your child's behavior on the field is not acceptable."

Regardless of what the coach does, you are ultimately responsible for teaching your child good sportsmanship. After the game, talk to your child about his behavior and, if appropriate, punish him. If your child is really misbehaving on the field, perhaps you should bench him for a future game.

Blueprint of a Great Athlete

IT'S HOW YOU PLAY THE GAME

Parents, coaches, and kids should define success as trying your hardest, not by wins and losses. Indeed, when a young athlete equates his self-worth with winning, it's a losing battle. A parent's reaction to winning or losing is really important. When your child comes home after a game, ask there are five questions you want to ask.

1. Did you have fun?

2. What did you learn?

3. How did you play?

4. How did the team play?

5. What did you do well?

6. What could you have done better?

Blueprint of a Great Athlete

TEACH YOUR CHILD TO ACCEPT

RESPONSIBILITY

When you lose, don't blame the officiating, the weather, faulty equipment, teammates, or some other factor. Athletes should accurately assess their performance, to acknowledge and take responsibility for their performance. It's also important to acknowledge superior skill in other players. Of course, there will be times when referees and officials miss a call. Remind your child that the officials are doing the best they can and that missed calls are just part of the game—and of life.

Blueprint of a Great Athlete

DISCUSS WHAT YOU SEE

When watching sports events with your children, take advantage of the opportunities to discuss what you see. Whether a player is arguing a bad call, kicking dirt, or simply cursing another player, you as the parent have a wonderful opportunity to talk about the situation, which is right and wrong, and how the problem could have been resolved without the negative type of behavior.

Likewise, there are a lot of good sports out there, so point out examples of good sportsmanship, such as the player who gives a helping hand to an opponent who has fallen down or a player cooling down a teammate who has lost his temper.

Blueprint of a Great Athlete

UNCONDITIONAL LOVE

Parents must demonstrate unconditional love for their children, and coaches must demonstrate unconditional respect for their athletes. They should say regardless of how you played tonight, that doesn't change how I feel about you as my son or daughter or my athlete.

With proper nurturing by parents and coaches, good sportsmanship can be accomplished.

Blueprint of a Great Athlete

ACTIVE WATCHING

Use spectator sports to teach sportsmanship

Whether you're watching a youth soccer game or viewing the World Series on TV, you can use what you see to discuss appropriate behavior. Here are some ideas to get started:

- When a player loses his temper, ask your child how the player might have handled his anger differently.

- When a player misses an easy shot or loses a key point, discuss what she does to collect herself and get back into the game mentally.

- If an athlete disagrees with an official's call, see if he lets his anger and disappointment throw off his game. Point out the consequences of moping over a call.

- When a player showboats after scoring, ask your child how she thinks that makes the opponent feel.

- If a player or coach is penalized for arguing with an official or fighting, discuss how the penalty hurts the entire team.

- Note examples of opponents acknowledging one another's good plays.

- At the end of the game or match, watch to see whether the players shake hands and part amicably.

Blueprint of a Great Athlete

ARE YOU A GOOD SPORT?

A checklist for parents and kids:

- Always play by the rules.

- Don't lose your temper.

- Cheer good plays made by either team.

- Don't talk trash or tease or goad opponents.

- Win or lose, be sure to shake hands with opponents and officials after a game.

- Don't yell at teammates for making a mistake. Never criticize teammates or coaches on the sideline.

- Admit your mistakes instead of making excuses or blaming others.

Blueprint of a Great Athlete

- Try your hardest on every play, even if your team is losing by a lot.

- Point out incorrect calls when they go in your favor.

- Don't argue with calls that go against you.

- Don't show off.

- Have fun!

Blueprint of a Great Athlete

Six Things Parents Should Say to their Player

For best results, parents should memorize and use the following:

Before the Match

1. I love you

2. Good luck

3. Have fun

After the Match

1. I love you

2. It was great to see you play

3. What would you like to eat?

Blueprint of a Great Athlete

Parenting Tip - Helping Kids Cope with Winning and Losing in Sports

Winning can feel fantastic. Being a good sport isn't about winning.

When children are 'good sports' they:

- are aware of other children's feelings

- say how well the other children did

- talk about the competition in a matter of fact way

- Listen to other children talk about the competition and how it felt for them.

Blueprint of a Great Athlete

Good sports' do not:

- put themselves down

- say 'It was easy' (it wasn't for some of the other children)

- boast and brag about winning

- make fun of the other team.

Parents can help children by:

- celebrating their feelings of success

- congratulating them on their effort

- being calm and happy

- reminding them of the other participants

Blueprint of a Great Athlete

- commenting on how different people might be feeling

- behaving like a 'good sport' ourselves

- telling them you love them whether they win or lose.

Some games seem to make bad winners and losers so avoid:

- taunting and teasing games

- grabbing and snatching games

- games where children push each other or hit each other with a ball.

Blueprint of a Great Athlete

Make your Child a real winner at Sports

Under the right circumstances, children and sports can be a dynamic combination. The most obvious contribution is to a youngster's physical development—improving balance, coordination and cardiovascular health. With a little bit of luck, an active youngster will grow up to be an active adult.

Sports can also affect a child's mental growth since mastering athletic skills can build confidence and self-esteem. Sports develop a sense of teamwork and cooperation for a child and teach discipline and responsibility. The lesson learned is that achievement in sports, like success in life, requires commitment and hard work.

Blueprint of a Great Athlete

Unfortunately, changes in our society during the past fifteen years have created conditions that occasionally make sports too stressful in today's world. Anyone who has observed a youth football, basketball, baseball or soccer game might walk away from the field thinking the phrase. Children participate in sports because they enjoy it, but some adults want kids to play sports for many other reasons—and that is where the trouble starts. Parents crowd the sidelines and fill the stands to cheer for their youngsters. More often they also yell at the coaches, officials and their own children. Grown-up officials blow their whistles with authority and often take the game away from the players. Coaches scream at the kids (and often at the referees and parents as well), berating them for bloopers and mistakes.

Blueprint of a Great Athlete

Parents and coaches should agree on realistic goals, such as beating your own record or improving some aspect of the game, rather than winning at all costs. That does not mean children should not be encouraged to win—but if a child has given his all, they can lose and still be successful.

The key to this philosophy is the belief that:

•Winning is not the most important objective and losing is not a sign of failure.

•Neither success nor failure depends on the outcome of a contest or on a won-lost record.

•Success is related to effort - you are never a "loser" if you have given your best.

Blueprint of a Great Athlete

What can parents do to make sure their child has fun playing sports? Begin by asking the child "How did you play today?" or "Did you have fun?" rather than "Who won?" Maintain close contact with the youngster's sports exposure to make sure all goes well. Be involved with the team —joining the parent's association or lingering before or after practice is another suggestion—not just dropping them off and picking them up. Do not look upon your child's participation in sports as a free babysitting service. By keeping in touch, parents will know early if their child encounters any problems, either physical or emotional. While not everyone can be a good coach or a good organizer, every parent can be an enthusiastic and responsible spectator.

Blueprint of a Great Athlete

Probably the most important things parents can do are to ensure that their child has a good coach. The right coach can make a child's sports exposure a good one, but the wrong one can ruin it—perhaps turning a youngster off to sports for good. Most youth coaches are just parents who give up their own time to coach the team. Parents can find out about a coach by talking to the coach's previous team's parents. I also suggest observing a practice, and talking to the coach yourself.

Keep in mind that a child's ability to run, jump, throw, catch or kick depends on their state of physical and intellectual development. Those who mature early and are coordinated will shine; those who develop slowly may be pegged as un-athletic. Competitive sports make superstars out of the children who play well and relegate the slow and awkward to the bench. Instead of learning to enjoy sports, the more slowly developing child becomes the spectator of later years.

In addition, recognize when a child has decided that organized sports is no longer fun. Studies have shown that one-third of all participating in organized sports drop out each year, and about 80 percent drop out for good between the ages of 12 and 16. This statistic alone should tell us that most children are not having fun playing sports. Do not consider your child a failure if they decide to stop playing. Try to find another interest or activity to take its place. There is nothing wrong with giving up baseball and taking up the drums.

Sports burnout has many physical ailments over a period of time. They display the following physical ailments that run the gamut from headaches to stomach aches to muscle aches. Many children exaggerate minor injuries so that they are not pressured into going back to playing. In addition, parents must also help children interpret the message they get from our professional athletes. The sports pages are filled with articles on pro athlete drug use or the most recent fight on the baseball field or basketball court. Parents need to talk to their children about the dangers of illegal drugs and steroids. Parents should encourage professional sport leagues to send a strong message to their children by banning athletes who use drugs and requiring random drug testing.

Blueprint of a Great Athlete

The Final Word

Parents need to do more than cheer from the sidelines to guarantee that their child has fun in sports. Perhaps the best thing a parent can do is to help fit the triumph and frustration of athletics into a balanced healthy life. It is really not that important how many medals and trophies a youngster brings home. He or she is your child first and an athlete second. Cheer your youngster on, but give the whole team your enthusiasm, win or lose, and let them know that it's not the score that counts but the fun!

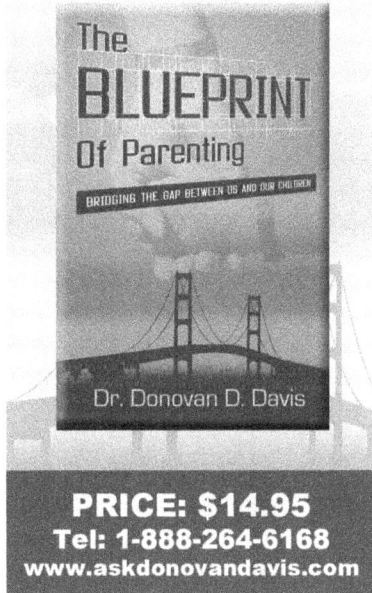

www.ingramcontent.com/pod-product-compliance
Lightning Source LLC
LaVergne TN
LVHW091206080426
835509LV00006B/865